MICHIG

PICTURE PERFECT PLACES

Mini Coffee Table Book

Welcome

Michigan, as a mid-west state, has the distinct honor of being nestled nearly in the middle of the Great Lakes. It borders on four of the five lakes and has a combined shoreline of over 3,100 miles. Within its boundaries lies a fertile land that nature has smiled upon and where people have thrived. Add a network of lovely rivers and sprinkle it with more than 10,000 inland lakes, include four distinct seasons, and you will find Michigan a state that just longs to be explored.

Changes were relatively slow between the ice age and the arrival of the first missionaries, voyageurs and traders. As the population increased, changes occurred at a much faster pace. Farms replaced many forest areas and cities were built. Shipping and the use of the Great Lakes increased dramatically. From the early lumber sailing sloops to the modern thousand-foot electronically guided ore carriers and countless recreational boats, the lakes have provided a living for some and a lot of pleasure for many others.

Lighthouses were built at strategic locations and harbors until there were well over a hundred of these stately structures lining the shoreline of the state. A few are gone but most of these historic landmarks remain standing and many are still in daily use. With the automation of the lights the lighthouse keepers have passed on, leaving behind their residences and living quarters, many of which are now museums.

Thanks to the wisdom of the founders and planners of

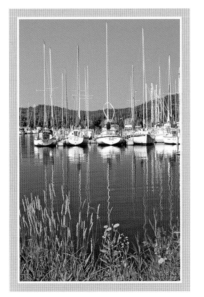

Michigan, there are vast national and state forest regions with thousands of acres open for public use. Many miles of pristine shoreline sweeps on to the horizon just as it has for centuries. One can watch the clouds of a Michigan sky draw imaginary figures on a soft summer day or feel the closeness of a myriad of stars on a crisp winter's night. Experience the mist and mystery of lovely sunrises and enjoy robust sunsets and the afterglow of the lingering twilight that follows.

Saginaw Bay, Sebewaing

Lake Huron Shoreline

Spray Falls

Upper Tahquamenon Falls

Grand Sable Falls

Lower Tahquamenon Falls

Munising Falls

Wagner Falls

Bond Falls

Grand Traverse Bay

Hart, Oceana County

Parent Lake Sunrise

Christmas Trees at Mesick

Presque Isle Light Station

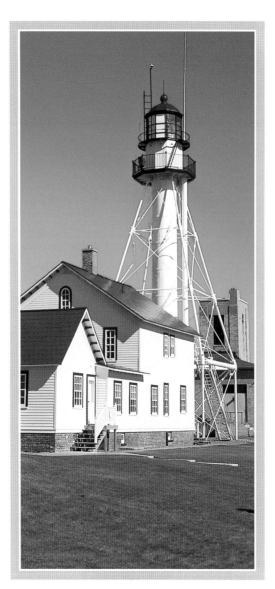

Whitefish Point Light Station

Tawas Point Light Station

Super Ship Indiana Harbor on Lake Superior

Silver Lake and the Famous Sand Dunes

Wind-carved Dune

Moving Sand Dunes

Little Sable Point Lighthouse

Patterns in Sand

Wind Sculpture at Work

Holland Harbor Lighthouse

St. Joseph North Pier Lighthouse

Michigan Lily

Bull Thistle

Evening Primrose

Goldenrod

Goat's Beard

Butterfly Weed

Autumn Birch Trees at Center Lake, Tustin

Northern Lake Michigan along Highway U.S. 2

Imp Lake, Hiawatha National Forest

Miners Castle at Pictured Rocks National Lakeshore

Tulip Time at Holland

Lake Superior View from Brockway Mountain   Brockway Mountain Drive, Copper Harbor

Lake Superior from Top of Brockway Mountain

Autumn in the Upper Peninsula

Fog at Sunrise along Lake Superior's Rocky Shoreline

October Colors, Mitchell State Park, Cadillac

Autumn colors in Michigan's Northern Region

Farm Market, Berrien Springs

Autumn Country Road

Autumn along U.S. 41 on the Keweenaw Peninsula

Grand Haven South Pier Light

St. Joseph North Pier Catwalk

St. Joseph South Pier Channel Marker

Winter, Lake Michigan at St. Joseph

31

Picturesque Lake Nineteen in Hiawatha National Forest

Sunrise over Lake Cadillac

Lake Superior, Au Train

Lake Michigan, Charlevoix

Rocky Northern Lake Michigan at Seul Choix Point

Manistee River

Two Hearted River in the Upper Peninsula

Observation Deck, Manistee River at Mesick

Crooked River, Alanson

Leland Harbor

Fresh Snowfall along Creek Road, Niles

Virgin White Pine Forest at Hartwick Pines State Park

Old Mackinac Point Light Station

Mackinac Bridge & Lightning Storm

Otsego Lake State Park

Warren Dunes State Park

Lake Superior, Alger County

Eagle River Shoreline

Sand Bay in the Copper Country's Keweenaw Peninsula

Lake Cadillac

Ada Covered Bridge

South Haven South Pier Light